Francis Drake

and the
Sea Rovers of the Spanish Main

John Malam

QEB Publishing

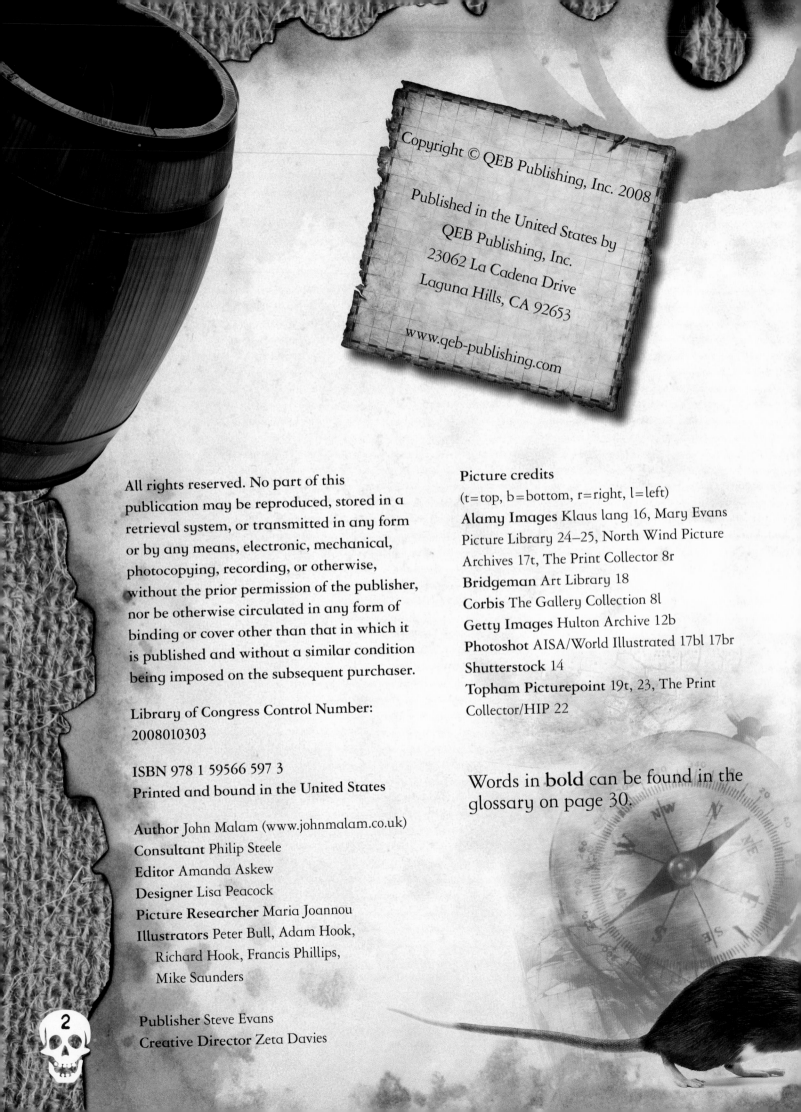

Library of Congress Control Number:
2008010303

ISBN 978 1 59566 597 3
Printed and bound in the United States

Author John Malam (www.johnmalam.co.uk)
Consultant Philip Steele
Editor Amanda Askew
Designer Lisa Peacock
Picture Researcher Maria Joannou
Illustrators Peter Bull, Adam Hook,
    Richard Hook, Francis Phillips,
    Mike Saunders

Publisher Steve Evans
Creative Director Zeta Davies

Picture credits
(t=top, b=bottom, r=right, l=left)
Alamy Images Klaus lang 16, Mary Evans Picture Library 24–25, North Wind Picture Archives 17t, The Print Collector 8r
Bridgeman Art Library 18
Corbis The Gallery Collection 8l
Getty Images Hulton Archive 12b
Photoshot AISA/World Illustrated 17bl 17br
Shutterstock 14
Topham Picturepoint 19t, 23, The Print Collector/HIP 22

Words in **bold** can be found in the glossary on page 30.

CONTENTS

Pirate attack!

In 1579, English sea captain Francis Drake was sailing in the Pacific Ocean in his ship the Golden Hind.

Drake was following orders given to him by Queen Elizabeth I—to explore the Pacific (west) coast of South America and raid Spanish ships and settlements. Drake boasted that "all the ships in the Pacific were in his power," and when he learned the Spanish **treasure ship** the *Cacafuego* had sailed from Peru loaded with gold, silver, and jewels, it became his target.

➡ *Despite being much bigger than the* Golden Hind, *the* Cacafuego *was easily captured by Francis Drake. It was an act that made him a pirate to the Spanish, but a national hero to the English.*

After a long chase, Drake caught up with the *Cacafuego*. The captain refused to surrender, so the English opened fire. **Chain shot** felled the **mizzen mast**, arrows rained down, and 40 of Drake's men went on board.

SHIVER ME TIMBERS!

Drake returned to England in 1580, where he was greeted as a hero. He kept some of the Spanish treasure for himself, some was shared with his **crew**, but most of it was handed over to Queen Elizabeth I.

The *Cacafuego* was soon in Drake's hands, together with a fortune in treasure. There was so much **booty** that it took three days to move it onto the *Golden Hind*. The haul included 13 chests of silver *reales* (Spanish coins), 25 tons of silver bars, 80 pounds of gold, and a large quantity of jewelry.

5

Pirates of the Spanish Main: 1550–1600

In the 1500s, Spain controlled much of Central America, the northern coast of South America, and many of the islands in the Caribbean.

This vast area became part of the Spanish Empire. It was rich in silver, gold, and gems, which were brought to Spain by fleets of **merchant ships**. The Spaniards had several names for their overseas territory, one of which was New Spain. Their English and French rivals had their own name for it—the **Spanish Main**.

SHIVER ME TIMBERS!

The Spanish Main once referred only to the northern coast of South America. The Spaniards called it *Tierra Firme* (the Mainland). From this came the English term "Spanish Main." Eventually it was use to describe the whole region.

Spain's empire in the Americas became known as the "Spanish Main." It covered a large area of land and sea, and offered rich pickings to pirates.

North America

Caribbean Islands

Caribbean Sea

South America

From about 1550 to 1600, the Spanish Main was the haunt of "sea dogs" from England, France, and the Netherlands. Many, such as Francis Drake, went there with permission from their governments to **plunder** Spain's treasure **fleets** and settlements. They thought of themselves as **privateers**, but to the Spaniards they were pirates. There was a fortune to be had by both sides. Spain looted the region's treasures and, in turn, the privateers—or pirates—took the treasure from the Spaniards.

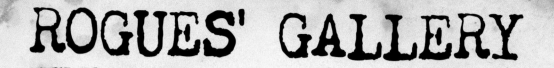

ROGUES' GALLERY

Francis Drake
Active as a privateer and pirate
1570–1596

John Hawkins
Active as a privateer and pirate
1562–1595

Richard Grenville
Active as a privateer and pirate
1586–1591

Jean Bontemps
Active as a privateer and pirate
1567–1570

Thomas Cavendish
Active as a privateer and pirate
1586–1592

Jean Fleury
Active as a privateer and pirate
1523–1527

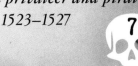

Privateers and pirates

When Francis Drake captured the Spanish treasure galleon the *Cacafuego* in 1579, the Spanish called him a pirate.

Drake did not think of himself as a pirate at all. This was because he had orders from Queen Elizabeth I of England to raid ships and towns that belonged to England's enemy. Drake was, to the English, a privateer. Whereas a pirate worked for himself and raided any ship he liked, a privateer worked for his country and only attacked his country's enemies. Drake was one of many English, French, and Dutch privateers who sailed to the Spanish Main in search of treasure for themselves and their rulers.

▲ *The Great Seal of Queen Elizabeth I was used to seal government documents, such as a Letter of Marque issued to a privateer. The seal showed the document was official.*

◄ *For much of her reign (1558–1603), Queen Elizabeth I of England was at war with Spain. She supported English privateers, giving them permission to attack Spanish ships and towns.*

Privateers were issued with Letters of Marque by their rulers. The letters were licenses that gave them permission to raid enemy ships and towns. As they were working for their rulers, privateers agreed to give them the valuables they seized. In return, they were allowed to keep a share of the **loot** for themselves.

The English government kept its share of treasure taken by privateers at the Tower of London—a fortress close to the centre of England's capital city.

SHIVER ME TIMBERS!

During the reign of Queen Elizabeth I, many English sea dogs did not get a privateering license. Francis Drake was one of them. He carried out his raids knowing that he had the full support of his queen, whether he had a license from her or not!

Treasure galleons

Treasure from the Spanish Main was taken to Spain by cargo ships known as galleons.

They were the main ocean-going ships of the day, with three masts, square sails, and several decks. Below the waterline were the cargo decks, where goods were stored in crates and barrels. Gold, silver, and jewels were kept in the treasure hold, which was the ship's strongroom.

Foremast

Forecastle

Bowsprit

Prow

At each end of a galleon was a tall section known as a **castle**. The **forecastle** was at the bow, or front, and the **sterncastle** was at the stern, or rear. The castles were fighting platforms where soldiers shot at their enemy with arrows and crossbow bolts.

Gunport

Galleon at a glance

Length: 98 feet to 147 feet

Width: 39 feet to 49 feet

Weight: 200 to 1000 tons

Speed: 8 knots
(9 miles an hour)

Crew: Up to 200

Cannon: 20 to 50

With towering castles, high sides, and many guns, galleons were top-heavy ships. They were difficult to maneuver and were easily rocked by the sea. Many galleons were lost in storms and some were picked off by pirates.

Ship's lantern

Mizzenmast

Sterncastle

Mainmast

Gundeck

Treasure hold

↑ A galleon was designed to carry goods, from everyday items to treasure. It was stored on the ship's cargo decks.

As pirates set about plundering the Spanish Main, Spain looked for ways to protect its ships and settlements.

Fortresses were built to guard ports and ships at anchor, but something else had to be done to protect ships on the open sea. From the 1520s, Spanish galleons heading home to Spain began sailing in fleets, guarded by warships. There could be 20 or more treasure galleons in a fleet, protected by heavily armed **escort ships**.

➡ *Richard Grenville and his crew attack the* Revenge *in 1591. They were outnumbered, so he surrendered. He died two days later.*

⬆ *Escorted by warships, Spain's treasure fleets crossed the Atlantic Ocean, taking their valuable cargoes to Spain.*

The Spanish treasure ships were loaded with silver from Mexico and Peru, gold from Ecuador, emeralds from Colombia, and pearls from Venezuela. After collecting their cargoes, the ships met up at Havana, Cuba, then began the long voyage across the Atlantic Ocean. It was difficult for a pirate ship to attack the fleet, as it was outnumbered and outgunned. All it could hope for was for one of the galleons to become separated from the fleet, as happened in 1585 when Richard Grenville captured the *Santa Maria*, with treasure worth at least $100,000.

SHIVER ME TIMBERS!

In just four years, between 1596 and 1600, Spanish ships carried treasure worth more than 34 million **pesos** to Spain— about $1 billion today.

Jean Fleury: Atlantic raider

Pirates on both sides of the Atlantic Ocean dreamed of capturing a Spanish treasure ship.

For the French pirate Jean Fleury, his dream came true in 1523. When he spotted three Spanish galleons off the Azores (a group of islands in the mid-Atlantic Ocean), he began his attack. He knew they were on the final leg of the voyage home to Spain, but had no idea what they were carrying.

⬆ *Aztec goldsmiths crafted beautiful objects, such as this mask. Spaniards wanted the Aztecs' gold, which they melted down and turned into ingots and coins.*

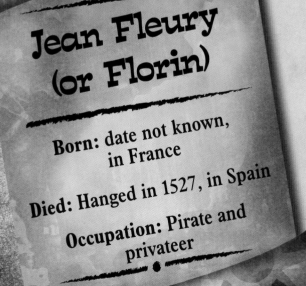

Jean Fleury (or Florin)

Born: date not known, in France

Died: Hanged in 1527, in Spain

Occupation: Pirate and privateer

After a chase and then a battle off the coast of southern Portugal, Fleury captured two of the galleons. He could scarcely believe his luck at what he found on board. The ships were carrying treasure taken from Montezuma, the last Aztec ruler of Mexico.

It was a massive haul of gold ingots, gold dust, pearls, emeralds, and jewelry. Montezuma's treasure had been on its way to the king of Spain. In 1527, Fleury was captured and sold to the king, who promptly had him executed.

SHIVER ME TIMBERS!

Fleury's haul also included live parrots and jaguars, and several tons of sugar, which was as valuable as gold.

▼ *No one was more surprised at the quantity of treasure than Jean Fleury.*

Doubloons and pieces of eight

In 1545, Spanish explorers discovered that a mountain at Potosí, Bolivia, contained a huge amount of valuable silver.

The Spanish claimed the silver for themselves and forced local people to dig it out. Before the silver was taken to Spain, it was cast into heavy ingots or struck into coins.

SHIVER ME TIMBERS!

In 1644, Spanish pieces of eight were worth four shillings and sixpence each in England (45 cents). In today's money, that is about $30.

A treasure chest used by the Spanish to transport silver. It was made of wood bound with iron, and was locked with padlocks.

◀ Safety in numbers. When Spain's treasure fleet sailed for home, it was escorted by warships. If a storm scattered the fleet, the treasure galleons became vulnerable to attack.

Spaniards called their silver coins pesos or *reales*. Each one had the number eight on it, meaning it was worth eight *reales*. Pirates had their own name for them—pieces of eight. The most valuable Spanish coins were made from gold, which the Spaniards mined in Colombia and Mexico. The gold coin was the eight *escudo* piece, which pirates called a **doubloon**.

▲ A Spanish silver peso, known to pirates as a piece of eight.

It has been worked out that the treasure on a Spanish treasure ship was made up of about 80 percent silver and 20 percent gold. A pirate who managed to grab just a handful of doubloons or pieces of eight was a rich man, but imagine how much richer he would be if he captured a treasure ship and all of its treasure!

John Hawkins: slave trader

The Spanish wanted to control the traders who took goods to the Spanish Main. The Spanish Main was their territory, so they decided who to trade with.

Although Spain and England were enemies, it was still possible for English merchants to trade with the Spanish, but the traders had to have permission from the Spanish government. John Hawkins did not have permission, but he still traded with Spain's **colonies** in the Spanish Main.

John Hawkins

Born: 1532, in England

Died: 1595, off the coast of Puerto Rico

Occupation: Privateer, pirate, slave trader, and naval commander

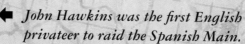

◄ *John Hawkins was the first English privateer to raid the Spanish Main.*

Hawkins was an English slave trader. He gathered his first human cargo in 1562, raiding Portuguese slave ships off the coast of west Africa. By raiding Portuguese ships, he became a pirate. He crossed the Atlantic Ocean and sold the 300 African slaves to Spanish settlers on the island of Hispaniola, in return for gold, silver, and pearls. Hawkins made another slave-trading voyage in 1564, again with hundreds of Africans seized from the Portuguese. It was just as successful.

⬆ **The** Jesus of Lubeck *was a royal ship loaned to Hawkins by Queen Elizabeth I. It was a large, heavy ship, which Hawkins used to carry African slaves.*

Hawkins was not so lucky on his next voyage. In 1568, his fleet of six ships was attacked at the port of San Juan de Ulúa, Mexico, by Spanish galleons. Only two ships escaped—the *Minion*, commanded by Hawkins, and the *Judith*, commanded by his cousin, Francis Drake.

SHIVER ME TIMBERS!

Hawkins almost did not make it back to England. The *Minion* was a leaky ship with little food on board. Of the 100 crew members, only about 15 came home. They survived by eating rats and parrots.

Privateer Weapons

A privateer's main weapon was their ship. It was usually a warship, smaller than a Spanish galleon, and armed with about 20 guns of various sizes.

There were large **cannon** that blasted enemy ships and ports with heavy cannonballs, and smaller **swivel guns** that fired **grapeshot** at other crews.

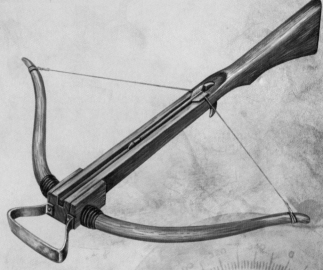

⬆ *A crossbow fired a short arrow called a bolt, which had a metal point.*

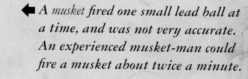

⬅ *A musket fired one small lead ball at a time, and was not very accurate. An experienced musket-man could fire a musket about twice a minute.*

For fighting at closer range, the crew used crossbows and firearms called muskets. These were guns with long barrels that fired balls of solid lead about 270 feet. If the fighting spread onto the ship, **rapiers**, daggers, and half-pikes were used in hand-to-hand combat. A **pike** was a pole with a sharp metal point at the end, used for jabbing.

For fighting on land, privateers used full-length pikes and **halberds**. A full pike measured up to 18 feet long, and a halberd was a spiked axe at the end of a pole. Some men wore metal armor on their chests and backs, but most protected themselves with **jerkins** —jackets made from padded leather.

↑ Armed with swords, halberds, and half-pikes, a group of privateers raid a settlement in search of plunder.

SHIVER ME TIMBERS!

Cannonballs were made from solid stone or iron. The smallest were about the size of tennis balls, and weighed about 16 ounces. The biggest were a little smaller than soccer balls and weighed about 64 pounds.

21

Francis Drake: the Queen's pirate

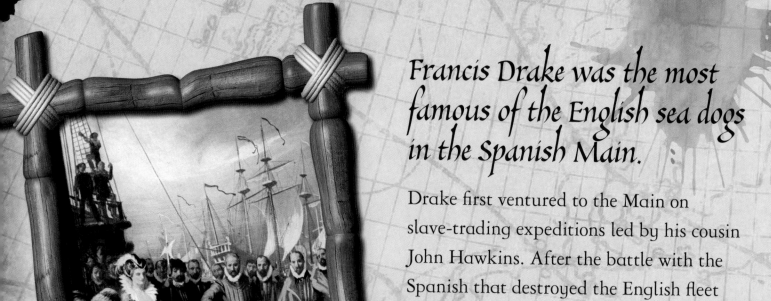

Francis Drake was the most famous of the English sea dogs in the Spanish Main.

Drake first ventured to the Main on slave-trading expeditions led by his cousin John Hawkins. After the battle with the Spanish that destroyed the English fleet in 1568, Drake wanted his revenge.

◄ *Queen Elizabeth I called Francis Drake "my pirate." In 1581, she went on board the* Golden Hind *and knighted him. From then on, he was Sir Francis Drake.*

Between 1570 and 1573, Drake attacked many Spanish ships and ports. In February 1573, he tried to capture a convoy of silver being carried to the waiting Spanish treasure ships. The attack failed. He tried again later that year, and took so much gold and silver that it was impossible to carry it all away, so he only took the gold. In England, Drake was greeted as a hero, and gained the support of Queen Elizabeth I.

In 1577, Drake sailed to the Main in the *Golden Hind*, with orders from the Queen to plunder Spanish property. It was his most famous voyage and it lasted three years. In March 1579, Drake captured the treasure ship *Cacafuego*, then sailed for England. He took the long way home, and ended up sailing right around the world!

Francis Drake

Born: 1540, in England

Died: 1596, in the harbour at Porto Bello, Jamaica

Occupation: Privateer, pirate, sea captain, and explorer

← *Francis Drake was the first Englishman to sail around the world. The voyage of the Golden Hind lasted three years, from 1577 to 1580.*

23

The Golden Hind

The little ship that took Francis Drake to success in the Spanish Main, and then went on to circumnavigate the world, was originally called the *Pelican*.

It sailed from Plymouth, England, in December 1577. Eight months later, as Drake prepared to sail around the tip of South America, he renamed the ship the *Golden Hind*.

Golden Hind at a glance

Length: 69 feet

Width: 20 feet

Weight: 100 tons

Speed: 8 knots (9 miles an hour)

Crew: 80

Cannon: 18

The *Golden Hind* was a warship, smaller than a Spanish galleon. Unlike bulky galleons, which had high sides and high-rise castles at each end, the *Golden Hind* was lower and sleeker. It could sail faster than a galleon and it was easier to handle.

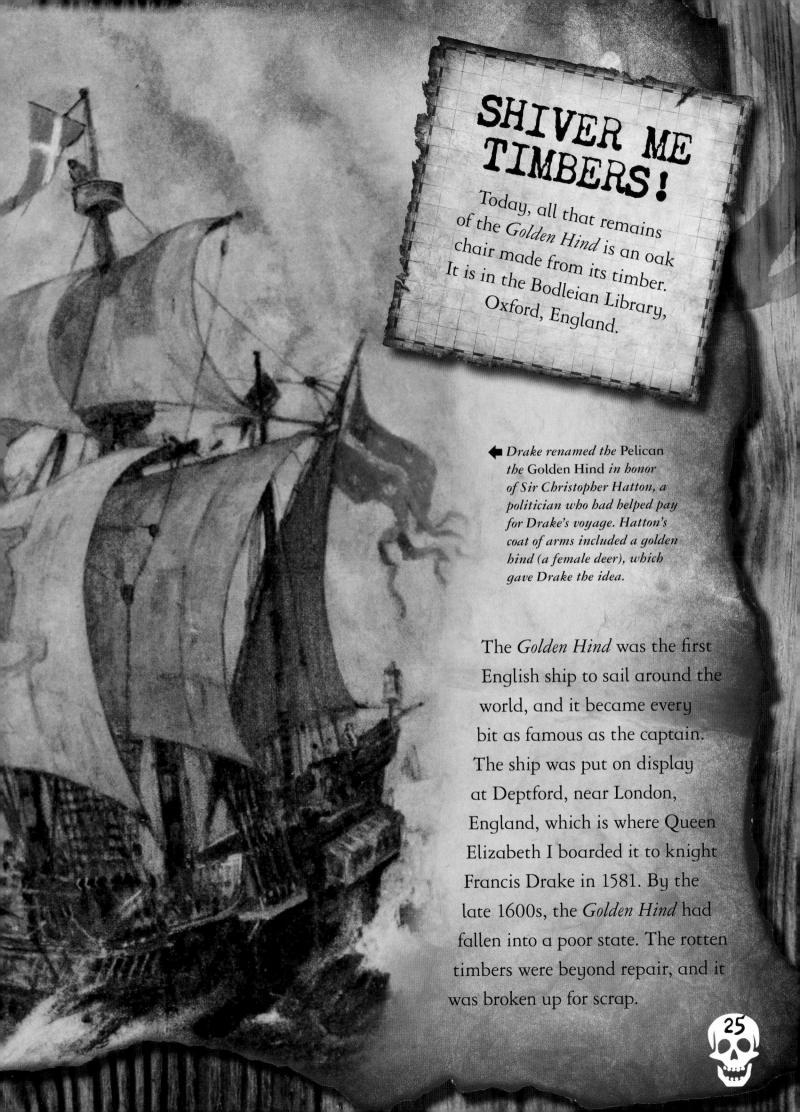

SHIVER ME TIMBERS!

Today, all that remains of the *Golden Hind* is an oak chair made from its timber. It is in the Bodleian Library, Oxford, England.

◄ *Drake renamed the* Pelican *the* Golden Hind *in honor of Sir Christopher Hatton, a politician who had helped pay for Drake's voyage. Hatton's coat of arms included a golden hind (a female deer), which gave Drake the idea.*

The *Golden Hind* was the first English ship to sail around the world, and it became every bit as famous as the captain. The ship was put on display at Deptford, near London, England, which is where Queen Elizabeth I boarded it to knight Francis Drake in 1581. By the late 1600s, the *Golden Hind* had fallen into a poor state. The rotten timbers were beyond repair, and it was broken up for scrap.

Drakes final voyage

Francis Drake sailed to the Spanish Main for the last time in 1595. It was also John Hawkins' last voyage.

The two cousins shared command of the expedition. They took 26 ships and 2,500 men. The plan was to capture Spanish treasure—but it did not work out. Drake and Hawkins argued from the start. Drake wanted to attack the Canary Islands, off the coast of north Africa, but Hawkins did not. Drake got his way, but the attack failed and some of his men were taken prisoner. They told the Spaniards about Drake's plan to raid the Spanish Main.

By the time the fleet reached the Main, the Spaniards were ready for the English. Drake wanted to attack Puerto Rico straightaway, but Hawkins thought it would be better to wait. Hawkins was sick, and while the ships were at anchor, he died.

SHIVER ME TIMBERS!

Drake had ordered his men to bury him on dry land. They ignored him. Instead, his body was put into a lead coffin and was buried at sea, the day after he died.

26

Drake went ahead with the attack, but the Spaniards fought him off. After that, he looked in other places for treasure, without much luck. A disease called **dysentery** killed many of his men, and in January 1596, Drake caught it and died. With both their leaders now dead, the fleet set sail and headed back to England.

▼ *The Spanish fortress at Puerto Rico was heavily armed, and Drake's attack was a failure.*

Jean Bontemps:
the fair weather man

Pirates from France and Holland also sailed the Spanish Main.

One was Jean Bontemps— a nickname meaning "good weather." He came from France, and in 1567, sailed to west Africa and collected human cargo. Bontemps tried to sell the slaves in Venezuela, but the Spanish settlers refused to trade with him. He sailed to Colombia, and on the way, seized a Spanish treasure galleon.

Jean Bontemps

Born: not known, in France

Died: 1570, in action at Curaçao

Occupation: Pirate

➤ *African slaves shipped across the Atlantic in the 1500s were sold to Spanish landowners in the Spanish Main.*

28

Bontemps managed to sell the slaves in Colombia, but only because he threatened to kill the slaves if the Colombians did not trade with him. On the return journey to France, Bontemps raided Spanish towns on Hispaniola and captured several ships. It had been a profitable voyage for him, but his luck did not last.

In 1572, Bontemps raided the Spanish island of Curaçao, off the north coast of Venezuela. About 70 men took part in the attack, but as it was pouring with rain, the **gunpowder** for their guns became damp and they did not work. Bontemps was killed. For once, he had not lived up to his nickname —the weather had helped him to get killed.

◄ *Jean Bontemps was struck in the throat by an arrow and killed.*

GLOSSARY

Booty
Goods stolen by thieves. Also called loot or plunder.

Cannon
A large gun or guns on wheels that fired cannonballs and other types of shot.

Castle
On a sailing ship, the raised platform at the bow, or front, and stern, or back.

Chain shot
A type of shot fired from a cannon—two iron balls joined by a chain.

Circumnavigate
To travel all the way around the world.

Colony
A country or area under the control of a more powerful country.

Crew
The people who worked on a ship. Also called the company.

Doubloon
A Spanish gold coin used in Spain and the Caribbean.

Dysentery
A disease that causes severe sickness, leading to weight loss, dehydration, and death.

Escort ship
A ship that protects other ships from attack.

Fleet
A group of ships sailing together.

Forecastle
The raised platform at the bow, or front, of a sailing ship.

Galleon
A large, slow-moving sailing ship used to transport goods.

Grapeshot
A type of shot fired from a cannon—a mass of small iron balls.

Gunpowder
A fine, black powder that burns easily. It was used to fire handguns and cannon.

Halberd
An axe at the end of a long pole.

Ingot
A block of metal, such as gold or silver.

Jerkin
A jacket made from padded leather.

Knight
To give someone the title of knight as a reward.

Letter of Marque
A license given to a privateer by his government or ruler, giving him permission to raid enemy towns and ships.

Loot
Goods stolen by thieves. Also called booty or plunder.

Merchant ship
A ship designed to transport goods.

Mizzen mast
On a sailing ship, the mast at the stern, or back.

Musket
A hand gun with a long barrel.

Peso
A Spanish silver coin used in Spain and the Caribbean. Also known as a piece of eight because it had the number eight on it, showing it was worth eight *reales*.

Piece of eight
The nickname for a Spanish peso or eight *reales* coin.

Pike
A long pole with a pointed tip. A half-pike was a shorter version.

Plunder
To steal, or goods stolen by thieves. Also called loot or booty.

Privateer
A person who has permission from his government or ruler to attack and steal goods from his country's enemy.

Rapier
A slender, sharply pointed sword, used mainly for thrusting attacks.

Spanish Main
Spain's empire in the Caribbean and the American mainland. At first it only referred to the northern coast of South America, but eventually it came to mean the whole of the Caribbean region.

Sterncastle
The raised platform at the stern, or back, of a sailing ship.

Swivel gun
A small cannon mounted on the edge rail of a ship, which could be turned from side to side.

Treasure ship
A ship used to carry treasure.

INDEX

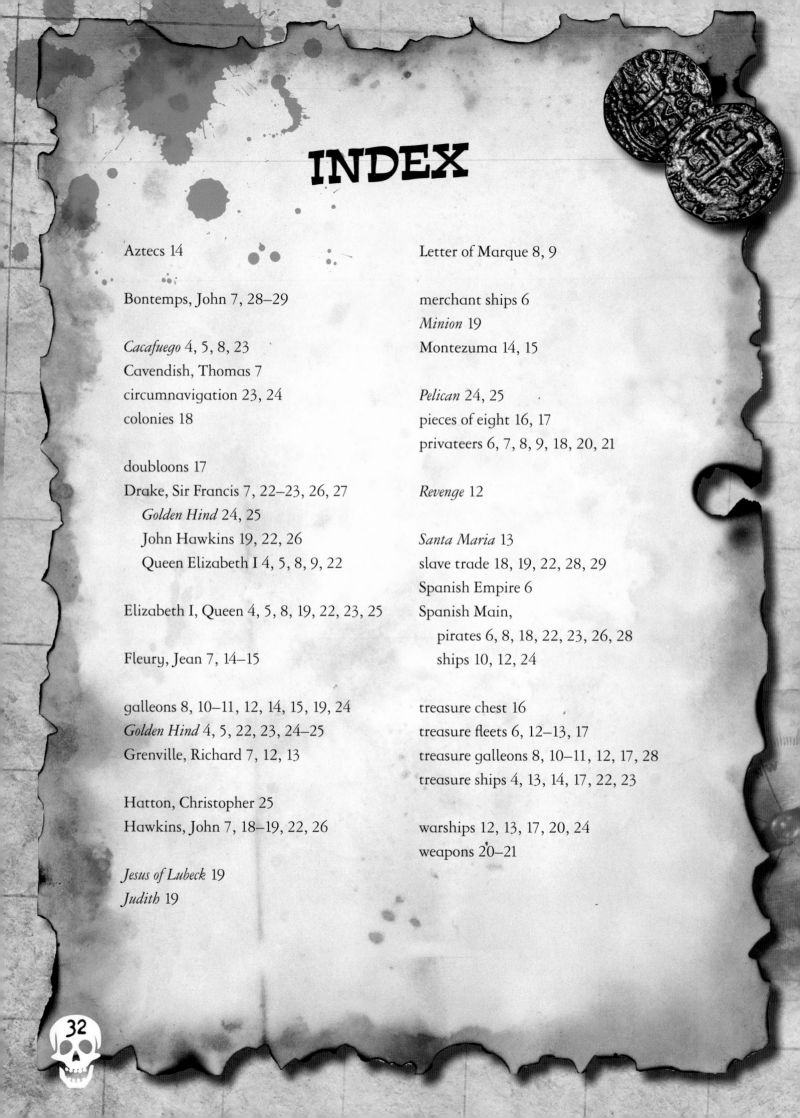